Delicious Brazilian Recipes

xxxxxxxxxxxxxxxxxxxxxxxxxxxxxxxxxxxxxxxxxxxxxx

Recipe 1: Brazilian Style Chicken Pot Pie

Looking for a dish that will feed your entire family? Then this is the perfect dish for you. Imitating an exemplary American dish, this is one pot pie dish that is stuffed brimming with Authentic Brazilian flavor that I realize you will fall head over heels with.

Yield: 10 Servings

Preparation Time: 1 Hour and 25 Minutes

Ingredients for Your Chicken Filling:

- 2 tablespoons of Olive Oil, Extra Virgin Variety
- 2 Onions, Medium in Size and Finely Chopped
- 2 Cloves of Garlic, Minced
- 2 Tomatoes, Fresh and Finely Chopped
- 2 Pounds of Chicken Breasts, Fully Cooked and Finely Shredded
- ½ Cup of Green Olives, Finely Chopped
-

1 Cup of Corn, Optional
- 1 Cup of Green Peas, Fresh and Optional
- 1 Cup of Hearts of Palm, Finely Chopped and Optional
- 1 Cup of Tomato Sauce
- Dash of Hot Sauce
- 2 Cups of Chicken Broth, Homemade Preferable
- 1 Tablespoon of Flour
- 1/3 Cup of Milk, Whole
- ½ Cup of Parsley, Fresh and Roughly Chopped
- Dash of Salt and Pepper, For Taste

Ingredients for Your Crust:

- 5 Cups of Flour, All Purpose Variety
- 1 teaspoon of Salt, For Taste
- 3 Eggs, Yolks Only
- ¼ Cup to ½ Cup of Water, Cold
- 3 Sticks of Butter, Cut into Small Sized Pieces
- 1 Egg, Yolk Only, Lightly Beaten and for Brushing

xxxxxxxxxxxxxxxxxxxxxxxxxxxxxxxxxxxxxxxxxxxx

Instructions to Make Your Filling:

1. The principal thing that you will need to do is utilize a huge measured pan and spot it over medium hotness. Include your oil and when your oil is hot enough include your onions and garlic. Cook until clear. This should take no less than 2 minutes.

2. Then include your tomatoes and cook for something like 5 minutes or until delicate to the touch. Then add in your chicken, olives, fresh corn, fresh peas, hearts of palm, fresh tomato sauce and your favorite kind of hot sauce. Mix completely to combine.

3. Reduce the hotness to low or medium and keep on cooking until your filling is thick and smooth in consistency. This should take no less than 10 minutes.

4. Add in your newly hacked parsley and mix again to join. Season with a sprinkle of salt and pepper and put away for later use.

xxxxxxxxxxxxxxxxxxxxxxxxxxxxxxxxxxxxxxxxxxxx

Instructions for Your Crust:

1. First add your flour and salt into an enormous measured bowl. Include your huge egg yolks and mix to consolidate utilizing a spoon.

2. Add in your spread and work it into your flour utilizing your hands. Add

some water gradually and keep on blending until a pleasant mixture starts to form.

3. Once your batter structures, envelop it by some saran wrap and spot into your refrigerator to chill for the following 20 minutes.

4. After this time preheat your broiler to 350 degrees.

5. While your stove is warming up cut 1/3 of your mixture away and save for sometime in the future. Carry out your outstanding batter and spot into a huge measured spring structure dish, ensuring that your mixture covers the side of your pan.

6. Add in your filling. Carry out your held mixture and spot over your filling, fixing both top and base pieces together. Cut two cuts into the highest point of your covering and brush with your egg yolk and water mixture.

7. Place into your stove prepare for the following 25 to 35 minutes or until brilliant brown in shading. Eliminate and permit to cool somewhat before serving.

Recipe 2: Classic Brazilian Hot Dog

This is a basic Brazilian formula you can make at whatever point you are searching for a delectable treat to appreciate. Easy to make and made with bona fide Brazilian fixings, this is one dish that is loaded with a Brazilian flavor that you will become hopelessly enamored with.

Yield: 4 Servings

Preparation Time: 45 Minutes

List of Ingredients:

- 2 tablespoons of Olive Oil, Extra Virgin Variety
- ½ teaspoon of Red Pepper Flakes, Crushed
- 1 Onion, Yellow in Color and Finely Diced
- 1 Green Bell Pepper, Finely Diced
- 1 Pound of Sirloin, Ground Variety
- Dash of Salt and Pepper, For Taste
- 2 Cloves of Garlic, Minced
- 1, 15 Ounce Can of Tomatoes, Finely Crushed
- 4 Hot Dogs, Jumbo Variety
- 4 Rolls, Large in Size and Brat Variety
- ¼ Cup of Parmesan Cheese, Freshly Grated 1 Cup of
- Bacon Bits, Crispy Variety
- 1 Cup of Peas, Frozen Variety and Warm 1 Cup of
- Potatoes, Shoestring Variety
- Some Mustard, Yellow Variety and for Drizzling

Instructions:

xxxxxxxxxxxxxxxxxxxxxxxxxxxxxxxxxxxxxxxxxxxxx

1. In an enormous estimated pan set over medium hotness, include your oil. When your oil is hot enough include your diced green peppers, onions and squashed red pepper. Mix to join and cook for something like 8 minutes or until your onions are translucent.

2. Add in your hamburger and season with a smidgen of salt and pepper. Cook for the following 8 minutes or until your meat is completely brown in color.

3. Add in your garlic and cook for an extra minute.

4. Add in your tomatoes, franks and a large portion of some your water. Mix to consolidate and keep on cooking for the following 15 minutes or until your sauce is thick in consistency.

5. Place a sausage onto each frank bun. Add some meat sauce over the top alongside a hint of Parmesan cheddar, a couple of bacon bits, a few new peas, a couple of potatoes and cover with some mustard. Rehash until each of your wieners have been utilized and serve while still hot.

Recipe 3: Grilled Beef Skirt Smothered in an Onion Marinade

Skirt steak itself is one of the most delectable cuts of meat you can appreciate. For the most delectable outcomes I energetically suggest serving this dish with some newly made Brazilian style cheddar bread or sound vegetables.

Yield: 4 Servings

Preparation Time: 4 Hours and 10 Minutes

Ingredients for Your Onion Marinade:

- ½ of an Onion, Yellow in Color and Chopped Coarsely
- 1 Clove of Garlic, Peeled
- ¼ Cup + 1 Tablespoon of Olive Oil, Extra Virgin Variety
- 1 Tablespoon of Water, Warm

Ingredients for Your Skirt Steak:

- 2 Pound of Skirt Steak, Skin Trimmed
-
-
-

Instructions:

1 teaspoon of Salt, For Taste
¼ teaspoon of Black Pepper, For Taste
Some Sea Salt, Smoked Variety and for Taste

xxxxxxxxxxxxxxxxxxxxxxxxxxxxxxxxxxxxxxxxxxxxxx

1. The primary thing that you will need to do is make your onion marinade. To do this place your onions, minced garlic, essentially ¼ cup of your oil and your water into a blender. Mix on the most elevated setting until smooth in consistency.

2. Place your steak into a huge measured Ziploc pack and empty your onion marinade into it. Coat on the two sides and permit your steak to marinate for the following 4 hours.

3. After this time preheat your barbecue to medium or high hotness. Eliminate your steak from the marinade and season with a smidgen of salt and pepper.

4. Place your steak onto your barbecue and singe on each side for the following 3 minutes. Eliminate from your barbecue and permit to rest for the following 2 minutes before serving.

Recipe 4: Brazilian Dutch Pie

Here is one more incredible tasting Brazilian style dessert formula that you will experience passionate feelings for. Debauched, crunchy and velvety all at the equivalent, this is one dish I realize you will not have the option to put down.

Yield: 10 Servings

Preparation Time: 5 Hours and 15 Minutes

Ingredients for Your Crust:

- 20 Squares of Graham Crackers, Honey Flavored
- 1 ½ Sticks of Butter, Soft
- 12 Cookies, Chocolate Covered

Ingredients for Your Cream Filling:

- 3 Eggs, Large in Size and Yolks Only
- 1, 14 Ounce Can of Milk, Sweet and Condensed Variety
- 1 Cup of Milk, Whole
- 1, ¼ Ounce Pack of Gelatin, Unflavored Variety
- ½ Cup of Water, Cold
- 1 ½ Cups of Cream, Heavy Variety

Ingredients for Your Chocolate Ganache:

- 1, 12 Ounce Can of Chocolate Chips, Semi Sweet Variety
- 1 Cup of Cream, Heavy Variety

xxxxxxxxxxxxxxxxxxxxxxxxxxxxxxxxxxxxxxxxxxxxxx

Directions for Your Crust:

1. The main thing that you will need to do is place your graham wafers into a food processor and mix on the most elevated setting until disintegrated. Then, at that point, move your scraps to a huge estimated bowl.

2. Add in your margarine and use your hands to cut the spread into your combination completely.

3. Press your piece blend into the lower part of an enormous measured spring structure dish. Line your cooked around the edges of your skillet, trying to squeeze them against your crust.

4. Cover with some saran wrap and spot into your refrigerator to chill for something like one hour.

Directions for Your Cream Filling:

1. First add your egg yolks, consolidated milk and entire milk into an enormous estimated pan. Set over low to medium hotness and heat your

combination to the point of boiling. Cook for somewhere around 10 minutes or until a thick cream starts to form.

2. Add your gelatin blend to this combination and mix until completely disintegrated. Eliminate from hotness and permit to cool completely.

3. Next whip your weighty cream in a little estimated bowl utilizing an electric blender until firm pinnacles start to frame. Include your cream combination and overlap delicately until equally incorporated.

4. Pour this blend into your spring structure dish. Cover with cling wrap and spot into your ice chest to chill for the following 3 hours.

xxxxxxxxxxxxxxxxxxxxxxxxxxxxxxxxxxxxxxxxxxxxx

Directions for Your Chocolate Ganache:

1. Use a medium measured pot put over medium hotness and add in your weighty cream. Cook for somewhere around 5 minutes or until your cream comes to a boil.

2. Remove from hotness and include your chocolate chips. Mix completely or until your chocolate chips are dissolved totally. Permit to cool somewhat prior to pouring over your cream pie.

3. Cover with saran wrap and spot into your refrigerator to solidify for somewhere around 60 minutes. After this time serve your pie at whatever point you are ready.

Recipe 5: Authentic Brazilian Style Black Beans

This is a genuine Brazilian formula that you will become hopelessly enamored with. Serve these scrumptious beans with a side of rice or one more bona fide Brazilian formula for the most delicious results.

Yield: 8 Servings

Preparation Time: 2 Hours and 45 Minutes

List of Ingredients:

- 2 tablespoons of Olive Oil, Extra Virgin Variety
- 2 Cups of Onions, Finely Chopped
- 2 tablespoons of Garlic, Finely Chopped
- 2 Bay Leaves, Fresh and Dried
- Dash of Salt and Black Pepper, For Taste
- 1 Pound of Sausage, Chorizo Variety and Sliced into Small Sized Pieces
- 1 Pound of Carne Seca, Soaked Overnight and Cut into Small Sized Cubes
- 1 Pound of Spareribs, Baby Variety and Sliced into Individual Ribs
- 1 Pound of Black Beans
-

10 Cups of Water, Warm
- 4 Cups of Kale Greens, Fresh
- 4 Cups of White Rice, Fully Cooked
- Some Hot Sauce, Brazilian Variety
- 1 Orange, Cut into Halves and Fresh

Ingredients for Your Farofa:

- 3 tablespoons of Butter, Soft
- 2 ½ Cups of Flour, Manioc Variety
- Dash of Salt, For Taste

Instructions:

1. In a huge measured pot set over medium hotness include your oil. When your oil is hot enough include your onions and garlic. Then add in your bay leaves and season with a dash of salt and pepper. Cook for something like 5 minutes.

2. Then include your frankfurter and cook for no less than 4 minutes prior to including your hamburger, spareribs, dark beans and warm water. Heat your combination to the point of boiling prior to lessening the hotness to low and stewing for the following 2 ½ hours or until delicate to the touch.

3. Remove basically ¼ of your beans and squash completely. Get back to your pot and season with a sprinkle of salt and pepper.

4. Place your kale greens alongside your white rice onto an enormous estimated serving platter. Spoon your blend over your rice and embellishment with your orange cuts and hot sauce.

5. Next make your farofa. To do this utilization a huge measured pan and spot over medium hotness. Include your spread and permit to soften prior to including your flour. Season with a hint of alt. Keep on cooking until gold in shading. This should take somewhere around 3 to 5 minutes. Eliminate from heat and pour over your completed dish.

Recipe 6: Brazilian Style Chicken Wings

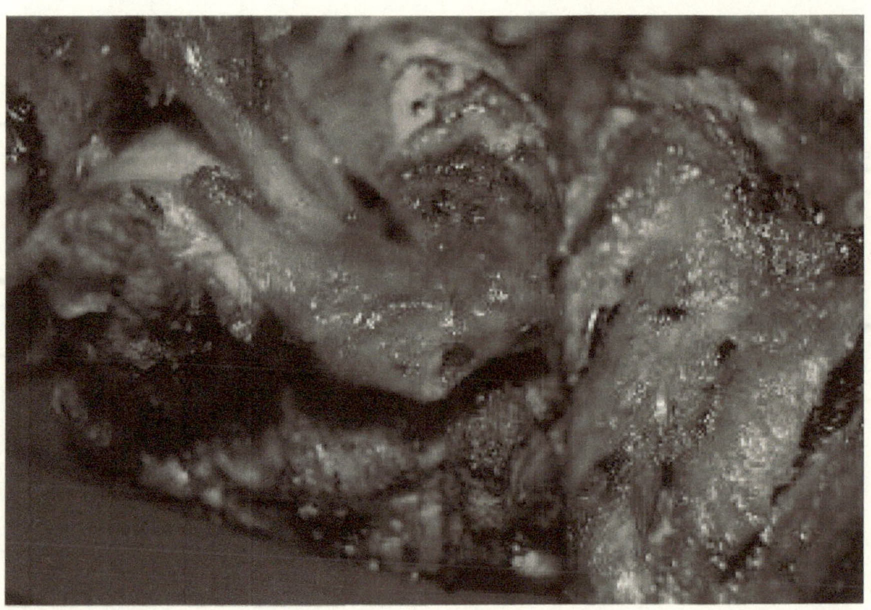

If you are looking for a dish to serve up just in time for the Super Bowl, then this is the perfect dish for you to make. Prepared with a tad of lime and garlic and marinated for the time being, these wings are exquisite, however they will leave your visitors longing for structure more.

Yield: 4 Servings

Preparation Time: 35 Minutes

List of Ingredients:

- 2 Pounds of Chicken Wings, Small in Size and Bone In
- 3 Limes, Fresh and Juice Only
- 5 Cloves of Garlic, Minced
- 5 Cloves of Garlic, Thinly Sliced
- ¼ Cup of Olive Oil, Extra Virgin Variety
- ½ Cup of Flour, All Purpose Variety
- Dash of Red Pepper Flakes, Optional and Crushed
- Dash of Salt and Black Pepper, For Taste
- Some Parsley, Fresh, Roughly Chopped and for Garnish Some Lime
- Wedges, Fresh and for Garnish
- Some Oil, Vegetable Variety and for Frying

Instructions:

xxxxxxxxxxxxxxxxxxxxxxxxxxxxxxxxxxxxxxxxxxxxxxx

1. Using an enormous estimated bowl include your new lime juice, minced garlic and run of salt and pepper. Then add in your chicken wings and toss thoroughly to coat in your marinade. Cover with some cling wrap and spot into your cooler to marinate overnight.

2. The following day place some flour into a huge estimated Ziploc sack and include your marinated chicken wings. Seal the sack and shake overwhelmingly to coat.

3. Then fill a huge measured pan with sufficient oil for fricasseeing. Place over medium to high hotness. When your oil is quite hot, decrease the hotness to medium and include your chicken wings. Fry until brilliant in shading. Eliminate and set onto a plate fixed with paper towels to drain.

4. Once your chicken wings are completely cooked spot onto an enormous measured serving dish and add some lime wedges around them.

5. Then utilize a medium evaluated pan and hotness some oil. Place over medium hotness and when your oil is hot enough include your garlic. Cook for no less than 1 to 2 minutes or until brilliant in shading. Pour over your cooked chicken wings.

6. Garnish with some newly parsley and squashed red pepper pieces in the event that you wish and serve right away.

Recipe 7: Brazilian Style Fish Stew

Here is a delicious stew recipe that you are going to fall in love with if you are a huge fan of seafood. Absolutely savory and packed full of a seafood taste that I know you won't be able to get enough.

Yield: 6 to 8 Servings

Preparation Time: 1 Hour and 10 Minutes

List of Ingredients:

- 2 ½ Pounds of Grouper, Red in Color and Cut into Small Sized Pieces
- 3 tablespoons of Lime Juice, Fresh
- ¼ Cup of Olive Oil, Extra Virgin Variety
- 1 ½ Cups of Onions, Thinly Sliced
- 1 Tablespoon of Garlic, Minced
- 2 tablespoons of Tomato Paste
- 2 Cups of Tomatoes, Roughly Chopped and Sliced into Small Sized Pieces
- ½ Cup of Fish Stock, Homemade Preferable
- 2 teaspoons of Salt, For Taste and Evenly Divided
- ¼ Cup of Piri Piri, Recipe Below
- 1, 14.5 Ounce Can of Milk, Coconut Variety
- 2 tablespoons of Cilantro, Fresh and Roughly Chopped
- Some Rice, Steamed and for Serving

Ingredients for Your Piri Piri:

- 1 Tablespoon + ½ Cup of Olive Oil, Extra Virgin Variety
- 5 Cloves of Garlic, Smashed
- 4 Chile Peppers, Cayenne Variety, Stemmed and Seeds Removed
- ¼ Cup of Lemon Juice, Freshly Squeezed
- ½ teaspoon of Salt, For Taste

Instructions:

XXXXXXXXXXXXXXXXXXXXXXXXXXXXXXXXXXXXXXXXXXXXXXXXX

1. Place your fish into a huge measured bowl and include your new lime juice. Mix to consolidate and permit to sit for the following 20 minutes.

2. Next heat up an enormous measured pot put over medium to high hotness. Include your oil and when your oil is hot enough include your onions and cook until clear. This should take no less than 3 to 4 minutes.

3. Then include your garlic and keep on cooking for another 30 seconds.

4. Add in your tomato glue, tomatoes, natively constructed fish stock and run of salt. Mix to consolidate and heat this blend to the point of boiling. When your blend is reaching boiling point make your piri. To do this hotness up an enormous estimated sauce container over medium to high hotness. Include your oil and when your oil is hot enough include your garlic and peppers. Cook for no less than 3 to 4 minutes. Then add in your fresh lemon juice and remove from heat.

5. After this time move your piri into a blender and season with a hint of salt. Mix on the most noteworthy setting until smooth in consistency.

6. Add your piri blend to your fish stew combination and coconut milk. Mix completely to combine.

7. Once your fluid is bubbling include your cut tomatoes and cover. Diminish the hotness to low and permit your combination to stew for the following 10 minutes.

Remove the cover and sprinkle your cilantro over the top. Season with a hint of salt and serve your dish with some cooked rice. Enjoy.

Recipe 8: Brazilian Chicken Croquettes

Here is one more totally scrumptious and divine Brazilian treat I realize you will experience passionate feelings for. These crunchy balls pressed brimming with healthy and generous chicken make for the ideal bite that even the pickiest of eaters will need to enjoy.

Yield: 30 Servings

Preparation Time: 1 Hour and 30 Minutes

Ingredients for Your Filling:

- 1 ½ Pounds of Chicken, Boneless and Skinless Variety
- 2 Onions, Medium in Size and Finely Chopped
- 3 Cloves of Garlic, Finely Chopped
- 1 Tablespoon of Seasoning, Poultry Variety
- ½ Cup of Parsley, Freshly Chopped
- 1 Pack of Cream Cheese, Soft
- 3 tablespoons of Olive Oil, Extra Virgin Variety
- Dash of Salt and Pepper, For Taste

Ingredients for Your Dough:

- 1 Potato, Large in Size
- 2 ½ Cups of Chicken Broth, Homemade Preferable
- 1 Cube of Chicken Bouillon
- 2 tablespoons of Butter, Unsalted Variety and Soft
- 2 ½ Cups of Flour, All Purpose Variety
- Some Breadcrumbs, Italian Style
- Bowl of Water, Almost Frozen
- Some Oil, Vegetable Variety and for Frying

Instructions:

xxxxxxxxxxxxxxxxxxxxxxxxxxxxxxxxxxxxxxxxxxxxxxxxxxxxx

1. First concoct your chicken and potato in somewhere around 8 cups of water. Include your chicken bouillon and cook over medium hotness until your potato and chicken are both delicate to the touch. Eliminate your chicken and potato. Save somewhere around 2 ½ cups of your stock and put away for later use.

2. Then pound together your potato and saved stock until smooth in consistency.

3. Place your stock once more into your pot and include your potatoes and margarine. Set over medium hotness and heat to the point of boiling. When bubbling include your flour and mix continually until a thick mixture starts to form.

4. Remove your batter and work for the following a few minutes or until smooth to the touch.

5. Next make your filling. To do this include your onions and garlic. Cook over medium hotness until clear. Then, at that point, include your cooked chicken, poultry preparing and new parsley. Blend completely until uniformly incorporated.

5. Season with a hint of salt and pepper prior to including your cream cheddar. Keep on mixing until uniformly incorporated.

6. Then make your coxinhas. To do this take a piece of your mixture and structure it into a little estimated ball. Level it with your hand and cause a little to bless indent in the middle. Spoon a spoonful of your filling into the center of your

mixture and close your batter around the filling, making a point to shape it like a teardrop.

7. Coat your coxinhas with a few water and roll in your breadcrumbs. Place onto a huge measured baking sheet and proceed with your remaining coxinhas.

8. Then fill a huge estimated pot with a liberal measure of cooking oil. Heat over medium hotness and when your oil is hot enough add in your coxinhas and cook until brilliant brown in shading. When gold eliminate and save to deplete on a plate fixed with paper towels.

9. Serve your coxinhas with some hot sauce and appreciate subsequent to cooling slightly.

Recipe 9: Tasty Grilled Chicken Thighs with Brazilian Vinaigrette Salsa

If you are looking for a classic and ultimately delicious dish that you can make to impress your friends and family, then this is the perfect dish for you. Totally filling and light, this is an incredible formula to appreciate without feeling remorseful in the process.

Yield: 4 to 6 Servings

Preparation Time: 1 Hour and 48 Minutes

List of Ingredients:

- 8 Gloves of Garlic, Peeled
- 8 Chicken Thighs, Boneless and with Skin On
- 6 Tablespoon of Butter, Fully Melted
- 2 teaspoons of Sea Salt, For Taste
- 1 teaspoon of Bay Leaf, Fresh and Ground

Ingredients for Your Vinaigrette Salsa:

- 1 Cup of Tomato, Peeled, Seeded and Finely Diced
- ½ Cup of Red Bell Pepper, Finely Diced
- ½ Cup of Green Bell Pepper, Finely Diced
- 3 tablespoons of Vinegar, White Wine Variety
- 3 to 4 tablespoons of Olive Oil, Extra Virgin Variety
- Dash of Salt and Black Pepper, For Taste

Instructions:

1. The main thing that you will need to do is preheat your barbecue to low or medium heat.

2. While your barbecue is warming up place somewhere around one clove of your garlic onto your chicken thighs.

3. Then utilize a little estimated bowl and include your spread, run of salt and inlet leaf. Blend completely until a glue starts to form.

4. Place your chicken into a huge estimated container with the skin side looking down. Place onto your barbecue for the following 7 minutes. After this time turn your chicken over and treat with your spread glue. Keep on cooking for the following 7 minutes.

5. After this time turn over your chicken again and treat again with your spread glue blend. Eliminate from your barbecue and permit to sit for the following 5 minutes.

6. During this time make your salsa. To do this utilization a medium estimated bowl and include each of your elements for your vinaigrette salsa into it and blend well to completely join. Spoon over your cooked chicken thighs and serve right away.

Recipe 10: Tasty Black-Eyed Pea Fritters

This is another Brazilian style road food that I realize you will not have the option to get enough of. Normally served during celebrations, this is one dish that will turn out to be incredibly well known in your household.

Yield: 20 Servings

Preparation Time: 20 Minutes

Ingredients for Your Acaraje Fritter:

- 1 Pound of Peas, Black Eyed Variety
- 2 Onions, Large in Size and Finely Diced
- Dash of Salt and Black Pepper, For Taste
- Some Oil, Red Palm Variety and for Frying

Ingredients for Your Filling:

- ½ Quart of Vatapa, For Serving
- Some Hot Sauce, For Serving
- Some Cooked Shrimp, Peeled, Deveined, Fully Cooked and for Serving
  Some Coriander Leaves, Fresh and for Serving

-

Instructions:

xxxxxxxxxxxxxxxxxxxxxxxxxxxxxxxxxxxxxxxxxxxxxxxxx

1. Place your peas into an enormous measured holder and cover with some water. Place into your ice chest to drench for the time being. The following day drain.

2. Place essentially ¼ of your peas into an enormous measured bowl and cover with some water. Wash your peas energetically to eliminate the skins. Once stripped, channel and spot into a food processor.

3. Add your onions, run of salt and run of pepper into a food processor. Mix on the most noteworthy setting until smooth in consistency. Move this combination into a huge measured bowl.

4. Preheat your stove to 250 degrees. While your broiler is warming up line a huge measured baking plate with some paper towels.

5. Then spot some oil into a huge estimated pot and spot over medium hotness. When your oil is quite hot diminish the hotness to low.

6. Roll your pea and onion combination into little estimated balls and drop into your oil. Fry for the following 6 to 8 minutes or until brilliant in shading. Eliminate after this overall setting onto your baking plate to deplete. Set into your stove to keep warm until all of your combination has been fried.

7. Place all of your serving fixings onto a huge estimated serving plate alongside your cooked pea blend and serve at whatever point you are prepared. Enjoy.

Recipe 11: Brazilian Style Cheese Bread

Here is a starter dish that you will go gaga for. Serve this dish with your super Brazilian course to truly bring it together.

Yield: 32 Servings Preparation

Time: 35 Minutes List of

Ingredients:

- 3 Cups of Flour, Tapioca Variety
- 1 Cup of Asiago Cheese, Freshly Grated
- 1 Cup of Milk, Whole
- 1 Cup of Oil, Vegetable Variety
- 1 Tablespoon of Salt, For Taste
- 1 teaspoon of Garlic, Minced
- 3 Eggs, Large in Size and Beaten Lightly

Instructions:

1. The principal thing that you will need to do is preheat your broiler to 400 degrees. While your stove is warming up oil an enormous estimated biscuit skillet with a

liberal measure of cooking oil.

2. Then utilizing a food processor include your custard flour, cheddar, entire milk, oil, run of salt, minced garlic and huge eggs. Process on the most noteworthy setting for the following 2 minutes.

3. Place your blend into every biscuit cup.

4. Place into your stove to prepare for the following 12 to 14 minutes.

5. After this time eliminate from your broiler and permit to represent something like 2 minutes before serving.

Recipe 12: Brazilian Style One Pot Shrimp Smothered in Coconut Sauce

Here is one more delightful and exquisite Brazilian dish that you will go gaga for. It is smooth in surface and is a definitive soul warming present for anyone who seriously loves shrimp.

Yield: 4 Servings

Preparation Time: 30 Minutes

List of Ingredients:

- 1 ½ Pounds of Shrimp, Jumbo Variety, Deveined, Shelled and Tails Removed
- 5 tablespoons of Oil, Vegetable Variety and Evenly Divided
- 3 Cloves of Garlic, 1 Clove Minced and 2 Cloves Chopped Coarsely
- 1 teaspoon of Salt, For Taste and Evenly Divided
- 1 teaspoon of Black Pepper, Evenly Divided
- ½ of an Onion, Yellow in Color, Peeled and Chopped Coarsely 1 Red Bell Pepper, Deseeded and Thinly Sliced
- ½ Cup of Tomatoes, Canned and Finely Diced 2 Basil Leaves, Fresh and Dried
- 2 tablespoons of Cilantro, Freshly Chopped 1 Cup of Milk, Coconut Variety and Canned
- 1/3 Cup of Chicken Broth, Homemade Preferable 2 tablespoons of Lime Juice, Fresh
- 1 teaspoon of Ginger, Ground Variety
- 1 teaspoon of Paprika, Sweet Variety and Optional 2 Ounces of Cream Cheese, Soft
- 1 Jalapeno Pepper, Red in Color, Optional and Thinly Sliced

Instructions:

1. First spot your shrimp into an enormous estimated bowl alongside your oil, garlic clove, run of salt and run of dark pepper. Throw completely to cover and permit to marinate for the following 10 minutes.

2. Then hotness up some oil in an enormous measured skillet put over medium hotness. When your oil is hot enough include your onions and diced chime peppers. Cook for something like 3 minutes prior to including garlic and cook for an extra minute.

3. Add in your tomatoes, basil and new cilantro. Cook for the following 2 minutes prior to moving to a blender. Put away for later use.

4. Add in your residual oil to your skillet and cook your shrimp for an additional 2 minutes. Flip and keep on cooking for one more little while. Move your shrimp to a serving plate.

5. Add in your coconut milk, custom made stock, new lime juice, ginger, run of paprika and run of salt and pepper to your blender. Mix on the most noteworthy setting or until smooth in consistency.

6. Transfer your mixed blend into a huge measured skillet. Heat this combination to the point of boiling prior to decreasing the hotness to low. Permit to cook for the following 5 minutes.

7. Add in your delicate cream cheddar and mix until completely softened. Include your shrimp and throw to cover. Eliminate from hotness and move to a plate. Present with

a smidgen of basil leaves, new parsley and a couple of cuts of your jalapeno pepper. Serve immediately and enjoy.

Recipe 13: Brazilian Style Empanadas

There is no bona fide and exemplary Brazilian formula very like this dish. It is unbelievably filling and makes for the ideal nibble to partake in any season of the day.

Yield: 20 Servings

Preparation Time: 1 Hour and 15 Minutes

List of Ingredients:

- 3 Cups of Flour, All Purpose Variety
- 1 teaspoon of Salt, For Taste
- ½ teaspoon of Turmeric
- 10 Tablespoon of Butter, Unsalted Variety and Soft
- 6 Tablespoons of Shortening
- 1 Egg, Large in Size and Beaten Lightly

- ½ Cup of Beer, Light Variety
- 1 Onion, Small in Size and Finely Diced
- 2 Tomatoes, Plum Variety and Finely Diced
- 1, 14 Ounce Can of Hearts of Palm, Drain and Finely Diced 2 tablespoons
- of Butter, Soft
- ½ Cup of Sherry, Your Favorite Kind 1 Tablespoon
- of Tomato Paste
  ½ Pound of Shrimp, Peeled, Deveined and Finely Diced Dash of Salt
  and Pepper, For Taste
  1 Egg, Yolk Only Some Oil, For
  Frying

Instructions:

1. Place your flour, run of salt and turmeric into a huge estimated bowl. Then, at that point, cut in your margarine and shortening until your blend frames a cornmeal consistency.

2. Next include your enormous egg and lager. Mix completely until equally combined as one. Cover and permit to rest for the following 15 minutes.

3. While your combination is sitting include your onions, tomatoes, hearts of palm and a dash of spread in an enormous estimated pan set over medium hotness. Cook for something like 2 to 3 minutes or until delicate to the touch.

4. Add in your sherry and deglaze your container. Then add in your tomato paste and continue to cook for an additional minute before adding in your shrimp. Cook for an additional 2 minutes. Season this combination with a sprinkle of salt and pepper.

5. Next add some oil into a huge measured pot. Heat over high hotness until your oil is channeling hot.

6. Roll your batter into even estimated balls and compliment with your hands to shape a round. Spoon something like 1 to 2 spoonfuls of your filling into the middle and overlay your batter over your blend. Brush the edges of your empanadas with a few egg yolks. Squeeze the edges to seal.

7. Place your empanadas into your hot oil and fry until brilliant brown in shading. This should take somewhere around 4 to 5 minutes. Eliminate and deplete on a plate fixed with paper towels before serving.

Recipe 14: Potato and Chorizo Packed Empanadas

Here is another empanada formula I realize you will not have the option to help yet appreciate. Go ahead and include your cherished sort of fixings to stuff your empanadas for the most delectable results.

Yield: 12 Servings

Preparation Time: 3 Hours

List of Ingredients:

- ¾ Cup of Chorizo, Finely Chopped and Spanish Variety
- 2 tablespoons of Olive Oil, Extra Virgin Variety
- 2 Onions, Finely Chopped
- 3 Cloves of Garlic, Finely Chopped
- ½ a Green Bell Pepper, Finely Chopped
- ½ a Bay Leaf, Fresh and California Style
- ½ teaspoon of Salt, For Taste
- ¼ teaspoon of Oregano, Dried and Crumbled
- ½ Pound of Potatoes, Yukon Gold Variety
-
-

Instructions:

1 Egg, Large in Size and Beaten with 1 Tablespoon of Water, Warm

12 Empanada Disks, Premade Variety

xxxxxxxxxxxxxxxxxxxxxxxxxxxxxxxxxxxxxxxxxxxx

1. The main thing that you will need to do is make your filling. To do this some oil into a huge measured skillet and set over medium hotness. Include your chorizo and cook for the following 4 to 8 minutes or until completely cooked through.

2. Next include your onions and keep on cooking for the following 15 minutes or until gold in shading and delicate to the touch.

3. Add in your minced garlic, new inlet leaf, run of salt, new oregano and diced chime peppers. Cook for the following 15 minutes or until delicate to the touch.

4. Add your diced potato into your onion blend and cook over low hotness for the following 10 to 12 minutes or until delicate to the touch.

5. Add in your chorizo combination and eliminate from heat. Mix completely to consolidate and save to cool completely.

6. Next make your empanadas. To do this preheat your stove to 400 degrees. Place your empanada plates onto a huge measured baking container fixed with some material paper. Scoop somewhere around a spoonful or two of your filling into the focal point of your empanada dish and overlap the mixture over, fixing the edges by pleating with a fork.

7. Brush your empanadas with your egg wash and spot into your broiler to heat for the following 25 minutes or until brilliant brown in color.

8. Remove from your stove and permit to cool somewhat before serving.

Recipe 15: Brazilian Style Pudim De Laranja

Here is a sweet tasting Brazilian dessert dish that I know you are going to fall in love with. It is the perfect dish to make to help satisfy your strongest sweet tooth and please those picky eaters in your household.

Yield: 6 to 8 Servings

Preparation Time: 6 Hours and 20 Minutes

List of Ingredients:

- 1 ¼ Cups of Sugar, Granulated Variety
- 2 tablespoons of Water, Warm
- 2 teaspoons of Lemon Juice, Fresh
- 2, 8 Ounce Cans of Milk, Sweetened and Condensed Variety
- 1 Cup of Milk, Whole
- 1 Cup of Orange Juice, Freshly Squeezed
- 6 Eggs, Large in Size and Beaten Lightly
- 4 teaspoons of Orange, Fresh and Zest Only

Instructions:

1. The principal thing that you will need to do is preheat your broiler to 300 degrees.

2. While your broiler is warming up set a huge measured pot over medium hotness. Include your white sugar, warm water and new lemon juice. Permit to heat up without mixing your combination and cook until your sugar completely dissolves. This should take no less than 5 to 7 minutes.

3. Pour your newly made caramel into an enormous estimated cake dish and twirl around to cover the base and the sides. Permit to cool totally until it hardens.

4. Using a huge estimated bowl include your consolidated milk, entire milk, new squeezed orange, huge eggs and orange zing. Utilize an electric blender and beat on the most elevated setting until completely joined. Empty this combination into your pan.

5. Add some water into a huge measured simmering container and add your cake skillet into this cooking pan.

6. Place into your stove to heat for the following an hour and a half or until the focal point of your cake is completely set and your cake is brilliant in shading. Eliminate and permit to cool completely.

7. Cover with some cling wrap and spot into your ice chest to chill for the following 4 hours. Serve at whatever point you are prepared and enjoy.

Recipe 16: Grilled White Cheese with Some Oregano Oil

These delightful sticks are commonly made utilize a thick white cheddar that I realize you will become hopelessly enamored with. Make these as a delicious bite or at whatever point you need to ruin yourself.

Yield: 2 Servings Preparation

Time: 1 ¼ Hours List of

Ingredients:

- ½ Pound of Cheese, Haloumi Variety and Cut into Small Sized Blocks
- 2 tablespoons of Olive Oil, Extra Virgin Variety
- 1 teaspoon of Oregano, Dried and Crumbled
- 6 to 8 Skewers, Wooden Variety

xxxxxxxxxxxxxxxxxxxxxxxxxxxxxxxxxxxxxxxxxxx

Instructions:

1. Thread your cheddar onto metallic sticks and spot into some virus water. Permit to douse for no less than an hour.

2. Meanwhile add your oil and oregano in a huge estimated baking dish and mix completely to combine.

3. Preheat your barbecue to medium or high heat.

4. Drain your cheddar sticks and wipe off with a couple of paper towels. Place onto your barbecue and barbecue for the following 3 to 7 minutes.

5. After this time move to your oil and oregano combination, making a point to cover it on all sides. Appreciate while channeling hot.

Recipe 17: Hearty Black Bean and Meat Stew

Here is yet another filling and hearty stew recipe that I know you won't be able to resist. While it may seem complicated to make in this recipe, the effort is well worth it in the end.

Yield: 8 Servings

Preparation Time: 3 Hours and 15 Minutes

Ingredients for Your Beans:

- 2 Pounds of Black Beans, Dried
- ¼ Cup of Olive Oil, Extra Virgin Variety
- 1 Onion, Spanish Variety and Finely Chopped
- ¼ Cup of Garlic, Fresh and Finely Chopped
- 4 Bay Leaves, Fresh and Dried
- 12 Cups of Water, Warm
- 2 Ham Hocks, Fresh

1. The principal thing that you will need to do is make your meat. To do this make your beans by add them into a bowl of water and permit them to splash overnight.

2. After this time heat up some olive oil in a huge estimated pot set over medium to high hotness. When your oil is hot enough include your onions and cook for the following 8 minutes or until translucent.

3. Then make your adobo. To do this utilization a little measured bowl and include your ground cumin, coriander, run of salt, run of cayenne pepper and adobo preparing. Mix to completely combine.

4. Add your garlic and dry straight passes on to your onion combination. Cook for the following moment before include your beans, your water, pork shanks and a big part of your adobo preparing. Heat this blend to the point of boiling and lessen the hotness to low. Permit to stew for the following 2 hours or until your beans are delicate to the touch.

5. After this time eliminate your pork shanks and shred your meat finely. Add your meat back into your stew and mix to combine.

6. Next utilize a huge measured bowl and include your frankfurters alongside your outstanding adobo preparing. Throw to combine.

7. Heat up an enormous measured skillet over high hotness. Include your frankfurters once

your oil is adequately hot and cook your hotdogs are brown in shading. When cooked cleave your wieners into little measured pieces and add to your stew.

8. Return your skillet back to high hotness add your hamburger and pork. Cook for the following 8 to 10 minutes for each until brown in shading. Add to your stew and permit your stew to stew for the following 30 minutes.

9. Remove from hotness and serve your stew with your hot rice and enjoy.

Recipe 18: Toasted Manioc Flour with Scallions and Eggs

Ingredients for Your Adobo:

- ¼ Cup of Cumin, Ground Variety
- ¼ Cup of Coriander, Ground Variety
- ¼ Cup of Salt, For Taste
- 2 tablespoons of Cayenne Pepper, Ground Variety
- 1 Tablespoon of Seasoning, Adobo Variety

Ingredients for Your Meat:

- 2 tablespoons of Olive Oil, Extra Virgin Variety
- 1 Pound of Sausage Links, Breakfast Variety
- 1 Pound of Sausage Links, Smoked Variety
- 1 Pound of Sausage, Chorizo Variety
- 1 Beef Tenderloin, Cut into Small Sized Cubes
- 8 Cups of Rice, White and Hot

Instructions:

Here is a dish that you can serve up to commend whatever other principle dish that you might serve up close by a fundamental dish that you are making. It is enticing and flavorful that you may simply need to serve this dish up yourself.

Yield: 4 Servings

Preparation Time: 15 Minutes

List of Ingredients:

- 2 tablespoons of Butter, Unsalted Variety and Soft
- 1 ½ Cups of Flour, Manioc Variety
- 2 tablespoons of Olive Oil, Extra Virgin Variety
- 4 Scallions, White and Green Parts Separated and Sliced Thinly
- 5 Eggs, Large in Size and Beaten Lightly
- Dash of Salt and Black Pepper, For Taste

Instructions:

XXXXXXXXXXXXXXXXXXXXXXXXXXXXXXXXXXXXXXXXXXXXXXXX

1. First add your margarine into a medium measured pan set over low hotness. When your spread is completely liquefied include your flour and cook for the following 8 to 10 minutes or until light gold in shading. Ensure that you mix continually as your flour cooks to keep it from consuming. Put away for later use.

2. Then utilize an enormous estimated skillet and warm up some oil over medium hotness. When the oil is hot enough include your scallions and cook until delicate to the touch.

3. Next whisk your eggs generally in a little measured bowl and season with a sprinkle of salt and pepper. Pour over your cooked scallions and scramble gently until your eggs are set.

4. Add in your toasted flour and mix completely to join. Season with some more salt and pepper.

5. Slide onto a serving dish and topping for certain more scallions on the off chance that you wish. Enjoy.

Recipe 19: Small Coxinha

This is a conventional Brazilian style road food is loaded with one key fixing: chicken. Indeed the actual name of this dish means little chicken drumsticks and makes for the ideal nibble formula to enjoy.

Yield: 20 Servings Preparation

Time: 40 Minutes List of

Ingredients:

- 1 Quart of Oil, Vegetable Variety and for Frying
- 3 ½ Cups of Chicken Broth, Low in Sodium
- 1 Onion, Peeled and Cut into Quarters
- 1 Carrot, Fresh, Peeled and Cut into Quarters
- 1 Rib of Celery, Fresh and Cut into Quarters

Ingredients for Your Chicken Filling:

- 1 Chicken Breast, Boneless, Skinless and Large in Size
- 8 Ounces of Cream Cheese, Soft 1 Ear of Corn, Kernels Only
- 2 Green Onions, Sliced Thinly 1 Clove of Garlic, Minced
- Dash of Salt and Pepper, For Taste
- ½ Tablespoon of Olive Oil, Extra Virgin Variety 2 Cups of Flour, All Purpose Variety
- 1 Egg, Large in Size and Beaten 1 Tablespoon of Milk, Whole
- 1 Cup of Bread Crumbs, Italian Variety and Plain Dash of Salt and Pepper, For Taste

Instructions:

1. Using an enormous estimated pot include your oil and set over high hotness. Preheat to 350 degrees.

2. Then utilize one more enormous estimated pot and include your onions, carrots, new celery and hand crafted stock. Carry this blend to a stew prior to diminishing the hotness to low.

3. Add in your chicken and poach for the following 12 to 15 minutes or until your chicken is completely cooked through. Switch off the hotness of your oven and eliminate your chicken. Permit to rest for the following 10 minutes.

4. Make your filling straightaway. To do this finely shred your chicken utilizing two forks and spot into an enormous measured bowl. Then add in your soft cream cheese, corn, minced garlic and green onions. Season with a sprinkle of salt and pepper and overlap completely to combine.

5. Strain somewhere around 1 ½ cups of your poached fluid, while throwing out the rest. Then use a large sized saucepan and place over high heat. Include your stressed fluid and some oil. Heat to the point of boiling prior to including your flour. Mix completely until a delicate batter starts to form.

6. Place your mixture onto a gently floured surface and manipulate for the following 5 minutes or until smooth in consistency. Carry out to at minimum ¼ inch in thickness. Remove little estimated rounds.

7. Place a spoonful of your filling into the focal point of each circle. Overlay the batter over and squeeze the edges together to seal.

8. Then utilize a little estimated bowl and whisk your eggs and milk together until beaten gently. Place your breadcrumbs into another little estimated bowl. Plunge each of your pockets into your egg wash first and roll in your breadcrumbs until full coated.

9. Add your pockets into your preheated oil and fry for the following 7 to 9

minutes or until brilliant brown in shading. After this time channel on a plate fixed with paper towels and serve while as yet funneling hot.

Recipe 20: Delicious Xuxu and Shrimp Smothered in Chile and Lemon

Here is a solid and new Brazilian style dish that I realize you will not have the option to get enough of. It's a distinctive looking dish that is pressed brimming with a new taste that you will not have the option to resist.

Yield: 4 to 6 Servings

Preparation Time: 40 Minutes

List of Ingredients:

- 6 Cloves of Garlic, Minced
- ¾ Cup of Onion, White in Color and Finely Chopped
- 2 to 3 tablespoons of Jalapeno, Fresh and Roughly Chopped
- 1/3 Cup of Lemon Juice, Fresh
- 3 Xuxu, Medium in Size
- 1 ½ Pounds of Shrimp, Large in Size, Peeled and Deveined
- ¼ Cup of Olive Oil, Evenly Divided
-

Instructions:

1, 14 Ounce Jar of Hearts of Palm, Rinsed, Dry and Cut into Small Sized Pieces
1/3 Cup of Cilantro, Finely Chopped

xxxxxxxxxxxxxxxxxxxxxxxxxxxxxxxxxxxxxxxxxxxxxxx

1. While mixing on the most noteworthy setting drop your garlic into a food interaction and cleave finely.

2. Then include your onions, jalapenos, new lemon squeeze and run of salt. Beat on the most elevated setting until hacked finely. Permit to represent the following 30 minutes.

3. Next strip the skin of your xuxu and cut into dainty estimated matchsticks.

4. Toss your shrimp with a hint of salt.

5. Heat up some oil in a huge measured skillet put over medium to high hotness. When your oil is hot enough include your shrimp and cook for the following 3 to 5 minutes or until completely cooked through. Eliminate and move your shrimp onto an enormous measured plate.

6. Add your xuxu to your skillet and cook for the following 3 minutes or until firm and delicate to the touch.

7. Return your shrimp to your skillet alongside your souls of palm. Cook for something like a little while or until quite hot. Eliminate from hotness and include your cycles jalapeno and onion combination. Mix intensive to consolidate and eliminate from heat. Serve while warm and enjoy.

Recipe 21: Chocolate Brigadeiros

If you are a huge fan of chocolate, then this is the perfect decadent chocolate recipe for you to make. These little chocolate balls are pressed loaded with chocolatey taste and shrouded in chocolate sprinkles. I realize you will adore these pastry balls.

Yield: 30 Servings

Preparation Time: 4 Hours and 15 Minutes

List of Ingredients:

- 2, 14 Ounce Cans of Milk, Sweetened and Condensed Variety
- 4 tablespoons of Butter, Unsalted Variety and Soft
- 2 tablespoons of Heavy Cream
- 2 teaspoons of Corn Syrup, Light Variety
- 3 Ounces of Chocolate, Semisweet Variety and Finely Chopped
- 2 teaspoons of Cocoa, Unsweetened Variety and Powdered Variety
- 1 Cup of Chocolate Sprinkles, Your Favorite Kind

Instructions:

XXXXXXXXXXXXXXXXXXXXXXXXXXXXXXXXXXXXXXXXXXXXXXXXXX

1. Using an enormous estimated pot and include your milk, delicate margarine, weighty cream and corn syrup. Then, mix to consolidate and heat to the point of boiling over medium heat.

2. Once bubbling add your chocolate and powdered cocoa into it and whisk well to completely join. Decrease the hotness to low and cook for the following 8 to 10 minutes or until thick in consistency, similar to the consistency of batter.

3. Slide your blend into a medium estimated bowl and cover with some saran wrap. Place into your cooler to chill for the following 4 hours.

4. After this time add your sprinkles into a little estimated bowl.

5. Then scoop your blend into little measured teaspoons and roll into balls. Roll your balls through your sprinkles and spot onto a baking sheet fixed with material paper. Rehash until each of your balls have been covered. Serve at whatever point you are ready.

Recipe 22: Moist Brazilian Coconut Cake

This delectable cake formula is one that you won't require a reason for to make. For the most delectable outcomes I energetically suggest serving a couple of cuts of this cake with a new mug of coffee.

Yield: 10 Servings

Preparation Time: 1 Hour

Ingredients for Your Cake:

- 1 ½ Sticks of Butter, Soft
- 2 Cups of Sugar, White in Color
- 4 Eggs, Large in Size and White and Yolks Separated
- 1 teaspoon of Vanilla, Pure
- 2 ½ Cups of Flour, All Purpose Variety
- ½ Cup of Milk, Whole
- 1, 13.5 Ounce Cans of Milk, Coconut Variety
- 1 Tablespoon of Baker's Style Baking Powder
- Dash of Salt, For Taste

Ingredients for Your Sauce:

- 1, 13. 5 Ounce Can of Milk, Coconut Variety
- 1, 14 Ounce Can of Milk, Sweet and Condensed Variety
- 2 Cups of Coconut, Flakes Only

Instructions:

XXXXXXXXXXXXXXXXXXXXXXXXXXXXXXXXXXXXXXXXXXXXXXXXXX

1. The main thing that you will need to do is preheat our broiler to 350 degrees. While your broiler is warming up oil an enormous estimated cake skillet with a liberal measure of cooking shower. Then line it with some parchment paper. Dust with a touch of flour and saved for later use.

2. Next include your huge egg yolks, white sugar and sticks of margarine into an enormous estimated bowl. Utilize an electric blender and beat on the most elevated setting for the following 3 to 5 minutes or until fleecy in texture.

3. Add in your vanilla and beat again to mix.

4. Next utilize a different medium estimated bowl and include your flour, pastry specialist's style baking powder and run of salt. Blend until completely join. Add this combination into your egg yolk combination and mix until uniformly mixed.

5. Use a different medium estimated bowl and include your egg whites. Beat on the most elevated setting with your electric blender until solid pinnacles start to frame. Tenderly overlay into your cake hitter until uniformly mixed.

6. Pour your pre-arranged player into your lubed and floured built up skillet. Place into your stove to prepare for the following 45 to an hour or until brown in color.

7. While your cake is heating up, make your sauce. To do this add each of your elements for your sauce into an enormous estimated bowl and mix well to combine.

8. Remove your cake from your stove and permit to cool marginally. When cool saturate the lower part of your cake with at minimum portion of your sauce. Punch holes over the outer layer of your cake and pour your residual sauce over the top.

9. Sprinkle a portion of your destroyed coconut over the top and spot into your cooler to chill for the following 4 hours. Serve after this time and enjoy.

Recipe 23: Brazilian Style Coconut Kisses

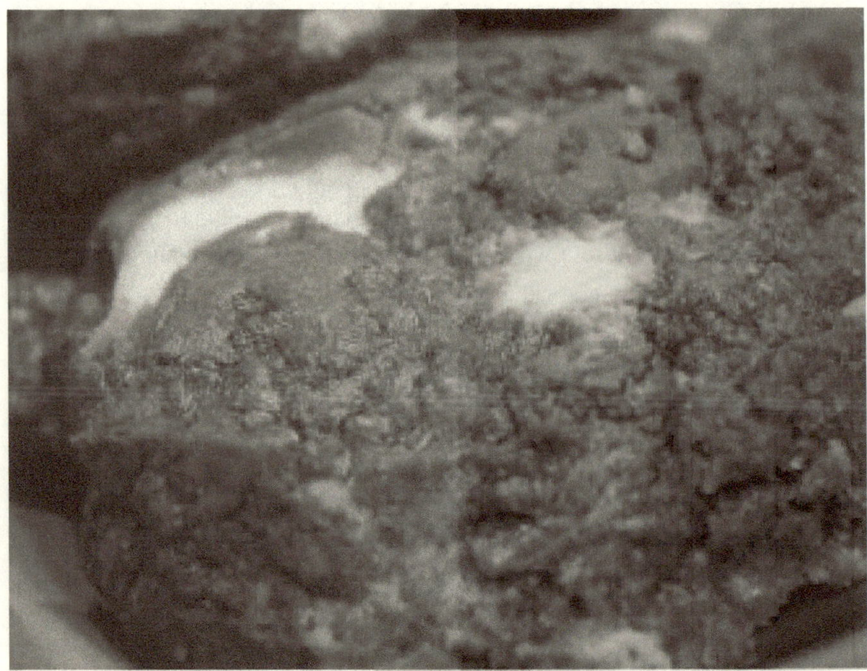

This tasty Brazilian dish is one that even the most amateur of culinary specialists can cook. It is a formula that main uses five fixings and additionally a formula can prepared in only a couple minutes.

Yield: 28 Servings Preparation

Time: 29 Minutes List of

Ingredients:

- 1, 14 Ounce Can of Milk, Coconut Variety and Condensed
- 1 Cup of Coconut Flakes, Sweetened Variety and for Dredging
- 1 Tablespoon of Butter, Soft and Unsalted Butter
- 1 Tablespoon of Vanilla, Pure and Optional
- Some Cloves, For Garnish and Optional

xxxxxxxxxxxxxxxxxxxxxxxxxxxxxxxxxxxxxxxxxxxxxxx

Instructions:

1. The primary thing that you will need to do is combine as one your coconut drops, dense milk and delicate margarine in an enormous measured bowl. Mix completely until equitably mixed.

2. Pour your combination into a medium measured pot set over medium

hotness. Cook for no less than 7 minutes or until your blend starts to thicken in consistency or until a mixture starts to form.

3. Remove from hotness and include your vanilla. Move to a liberally lubed plate. Permit to cool completely.

4. Once your blend is cool roll into even measured balls and dig them in your coconut chips until totally covered.

5. Place your balls into little estimated paper bonbon cups. Finish with your entire cloves squarely in the middle and appreciate at whatever point you are ready.

Recipe 24: Healthy Passion Fruit Mousse

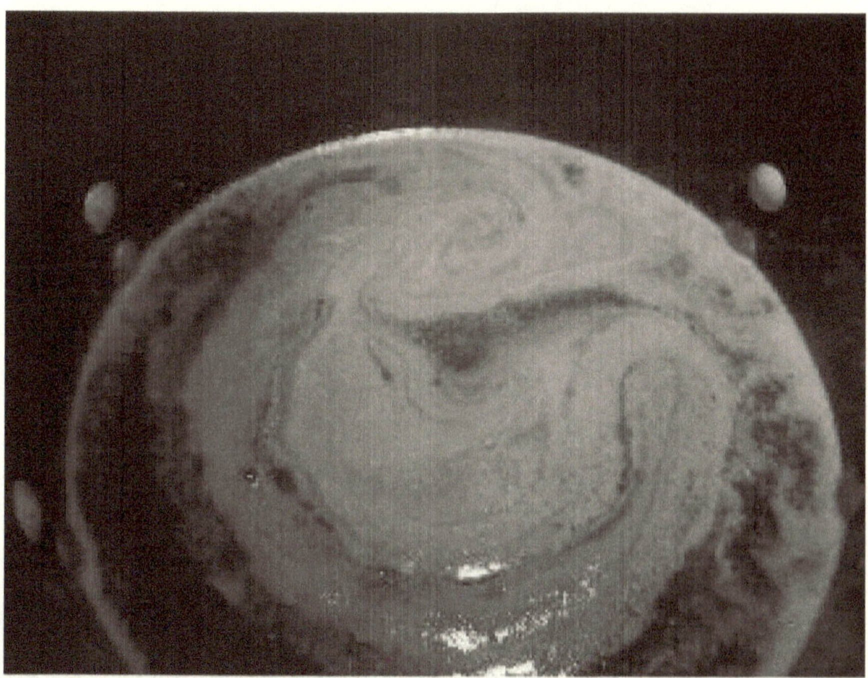

This is an amazingly simple and tasty South American sweet dish that I realize you will need to make again and again. This ordinary Brazilian mousse dish is made with new energy organic product, some whipping cream and sugar, making it a definitive method for fulfilling your sweet tooth cravings.

Yield: 15 to 20 Servings

Preparation Time:

List of Ingredients:

- 2 Envelopes of Gelatin,
- ¼ Cup of Water, Warm
- 1 ½ Cups of Passion Fruit, Concentrated Variety and Unsweetened
- 1 Tablespoon of Lime Juice, Fresh
- 1 + 2/3 Cups of Cream, Heavy Whipping Variety
- 6 Eggs, Large in Size and Whites Only
- 1/3 teaspoons of Cream of Tartar
- 2 Cups of Sugar, White in Color
- 2 to 3 Passion Fruits, Pulp, Seeds and Optional

Ingredients for Your Garnishes:

- 6 Passion Fruits, Pulp Only
- Some Whipped Cream
- Some Passion Fruit, Sorbet Variety

Instructions:

XXXXXXXXXXXXXXXXXXXXXXXXXXXXXXXXXXXXXXXXXXXXXXXXXX

1. Use an enormous estimated pan set over medium hotness and include your enthusiasm natural product juice and new lime juice. Mix completely to join and cook for the following a few minutes or until your sugar completely disintegrates. When disintegrated eliminate from hotness and permit to cool completely.

2. Then spot your gelatin into your water and mix to blend. Permit to break up complete and turn out to be delicate. This should require something like 5 minutes. Mix into your enthusiasm natural product combination until completely incorporated.

3. Allow your blend to cool for the following 30 minutes.

4. Next empty your weighty cream into a little measured bowl and beat with an electric combination on the most elevated setting until firm pinnacles start to frame. Delicately overlap into your enthusiasm organic product combination until uniformly incorporated.

5. Add your egg whites and cream of tartar into a little measured bowl and beat with an electric blender on the most noteworthy setting until solid pinnacles start to frame. Add your egg white combination into your energy natural product blend and mix completely to combine.

6. Pour your combination into a treat shape. Cover with some saran wrap and spot into your cooler to chill for something like 6 to 8 hours.

7. After this time eliminate from your pastry milk and present with a fixing of some energy organic product mash on top just as all of your trimming ingredients.

Recipe 25: Traditional Brazilian Flan

While flan itself might be viewed as an exemplary Spanish treat dish, there could be no other flan formula very like this one. It is not difficult to make and just requires a couple of fixings to put together.

Yield: 8 Servings

Preparation Time: 9 Hours and 30 Minutes

List of Ingredients:

- 1 Cup of Sugar, White in Color
- 1/3 Cup of Water, Warm
- 2, 14 Ounce Cans of Milk, Sweet and Condensed Variety
- 28 Ounces of Milk, Whole
- 4 Eggs, Large in Size
- 1 Tablespoon of Vanilla, Pure

Instructions:

xxxxxxxxxxxxxxxxxxxxxxxxxxxxxxxxxxxxxxxxxxxxxxxxxx

1. The primary thing that you will need to do is preheat your broiler to 375 degrees.

2. While your stove is warming up utilize an enormous estimated pan and set over medium to high hotness. Include your sugar and cook for somewhere around 10 minutes or until brilliant brown in shading. Ensure that you mix completely as it cooks and permit it to turn out to be thick in consistency.

3. Pour this blend into a little measured cake skillet and twirl your container to ensure it covers the base and the sides. Permit your combination to sit for no less than a couple of moments or until it hardens.

4. Add in your dense milk, entire milk, huge eggs and unadulterated vanilla into a blender. Mix on the most noteworthy setting for the following 2 to 3 minutes or until smooth in consistency. Empty this combination into your cake container and cover with some aluminum foil.

5. Next top off a huge measured baking dish with some water and spot your flan skillet into it.

6. Place into your broiler and permit to heat for the following hour and 30 minutes or until the highest point of your flan is brilliant in color.

7. Remove from your stove and permit to cool totally. Place into your ice chest to chill for the time being and serve at whatever point you are ready.

Author's Afterthoughts

Thank you to every one of the perusers who put time and cash into my book! I esteem all of you and trust you enjoyed a similar perusing it as I did recorded as a hard copy it.

Out of each of the books out there, you picked dig and for that I am really appreciative. It puts forth the attempt worth the effort when I realize my perusers are partaking in my work from start to finish.